"LESSONS LEARNED"

Tales from the Woodshed and Beyond

By Ron and Mary Achterkirch

To Jim,

the best of brothers!

Our love, Mary & Ron

This book celebrates our love for God and our love for family. 1st John, chapters 4 and 5, gives us answers to many questions such as "How then should we live?" Loving God means keeping his commandments. He has given us eternal life and this life is in the Son.

May we live in fellowship with the true God and with his son, Jesus for he is the only true God and He is eternal life.

"LESSONS LEARNED"

Tales from the Woodshed and Beyond

Ron and Mary, who lived these stories.

To Those Who It Is Written For:

This book is dedicated to and written for our grandchildren.

Rueben G. Achterkirch
Irene I Clement

Ronald Achterkirch

Louis Bergtold
Louise Losen

Mary Bergtold

Ian Achterkirch
Christine Ummel

Meredith Achterkirch
Peter Achterkirch
Charlotte Achterkirch
Claire Achterkirch
David Achterkirch

Amy Achterkirch Berger
Michael Berger

Kael Berger
Kirra Berger

Our grandchildren, for whom this book is written.

CONTENTS

ACKNOWLEGEMENTS

Thank you to Davon Harris who transcribed hours of voice recordings, Terri Hands, who initiated the idea of the book and Al Edeker, who facilitated the process.

Art work for the book front and back covers is by our talented friend Millie Johnson and is used with her permission.

FORWARD

Who is that knocking at the door at 8:00 am on a cold November Minnesota morning? It was a total stranger who had owned and totally remodeled this home 10 years earlier! He saw our campaign signs out in "Our Yard" and had to meet us!

What brave, friendly soul does that? Ron Achterkirch, that's who! And boy, are we glad he did!

We have met him and his Saint of a "bride" Mary, who we now see once or twice a month! Ron is one of the most visionary, driven, action oriented, highly effective, hysterical, leaders that I have ever met. Plus he has a heart of gold!

In getting to know them, they have some of the funniest and most interesting stories in their exceptionally, adventurous lives. I think that it is interesting that you can sit next to someone in their 70's or older at church and have no idea the fascinating, spellbinding stories they could tell!! Ron and Mary are two of those!

One day, when they were at "Our Home," I suggested they tell their stories in a book. And that is what they have done in this one. It is easy, light hearted, fun reading about a very brave, adventurous couple who have lived their lives to the fullest. They are Christians who show us how Jesus was always right there in the midst of this sweet couple's lives!

Terri Hands

PROLOGUE

You cannot make this stuff up. These are real stories and events that I and my wife Mary experienced in our fifty-eight years of marriage. We have lived on four of the seven continents, and traveled to a fifth. Each story taught us a God Given lesson that we have found useful.

One day I was driving down the street that Mary and I had lived on for thirty plus years. I noticed that our house and its front yard were festooned with political signs of the same ilk I would have had. I decided to stop in and introduce myself to the new owners of our "house". My intent was to let them know that I felt that the home was in good hands. The door was answered by Terri Hands. She introduced me to her husband George. We have since become friends. Terri is my main encourager in doing this book.

I believe that God brought them to this home so that we would meet. The Hands hold a strong faith in our Lord.

The constants in our lives are God and His Church, our marriage and family, and a pet cat. Mary and I have been together for 58 years as of this writing. With these constants, we have moved around the world, raised two great kids, and lived these stories.

This book of lessons is a gift from God dedicated to our grandchildren - a legacy. A modern book of lore.

THE UNIVERSE IS MADE OF STORIES NOT ATOMS (MURIEL RUKEYSER - POET)

FAITH: FOUNDATIONS

I have learned over the decades that the truths of God are my strength and foundation. I have learned to lean into this strength through the stories as told here. As I continued my walk with The Lord, I saw how in many ways He was always in our stories.

We encapsulated these truths in the lessons that we have lived as written in this book.

FAITH: FOUNDATIONS

LESSON

LIFE

Looking back at these stories, we are reminded of the number of times God reached down and brought good to our life. These stories are just some of those times.

Each story taught me a lesson that I have used in my life.

GOD IS GOOD

Lesson: God Is Good and can make good things come from bad.

Romans 8: 28. And we know that God causes everything to work together for the good of those who love God and are called according to his purpose for them. NLT

FAITH: FOUNDATIONS

LESSON

LOVE

God revealed his character to me through these lessons.

GOD IS LOVE

Lesson: He is crazy in love with you.

> Pastor Brad Kindall
> Faith Covenant Church, Burnsville, MN

1 John 4:16. We know how much God loves us, and we have put our trust in his love. God is love, and all who live in love live in God, and God lives in them. NLT

FAITH: FOUNDATIONS

LESSON

VOLUNTEER WORKERS

Churches and 501 C-3 organizations depend on many volunteers to do their work. The good ones are worth their weight in gold, the bad ones really slow you up.

I experienced this truth as a member of the church councils that I was a member of. In more than one case the church kitchen was run by a volunteer. After some period of time the person running the kitchen began to think that the kitchen was their personal property. They would make up rules without council approval or consultation. In all cases removing the person was incredibly messy.

Lesson: It is really hard to fire an incompetent worker in a volunteer organization.

FAITH: FOUNDATIONS

LESSON

KNOW YOURSELF

WHEN YOU KNOW WHO YOU ARE, YOU KNOW WHAT TO DO

(Pastor Brad Kindall. Burnsville MN)

When we lived in Brussels I was a product line sales manager. I had responsibility for sixteen countries for that product line. Once I was traveling with my boss and were in Stockholm Sweden where prostitution was legal and common. At the end of the evening and on our way to our rooms my boss asked me to set him up with one of the prostitutes and send her to his room. I DID NOT DO THIS.

Lesson: Learn who you are.

FAITH: FOUNDATIONS

LESSON

GIVING

We were members of King of Glory Lutheran Church in Fountain Valley California. I was chair of the congregation. We gave five dollars a week, which I thought was a princely sum. Our Pastor, Harvey, kept challenging Mary and me to tithe. We decided to give it a try. I was almost physically ill when I wrote the check out for 10% of our income. That was a lot of money, around $100.00. We stuck with it for the next few months and realized that our income had increased significantly. And, to our surprise, that following year our income doubled.

Lesson: You cannot out give The LORD.

2 Corinthians 9:6,8 Remember this—a farmer who plants only a few seeds will get a small crop. But the one who plants generously will get a generous crop. NLT

FAITH: FOUNDATIONS

LESSON

WORDS TO LIVE BY

WELL DONE GOOD AND FAITHFUL SERVANT

In my study of the scriptures, discussions with fellow Christians, and 80 years of Sunday sermons I have learned that we live according to our belief system. Living this life then leaves footprints. These footprints are who we are. When we meet The Lord he will verify that our life was lived for Him by Him stating, "Well done good and faithful servant."

Lesson: These words are all you need to hear when you meet the Lord.

GROWING UP

GROWING UP

LESSON

PARENT RESPONSIBILITY - RON

Growing up there were six people in my family. Dad (Reuben, by name and 100% German by birth), Mom (50% Swede and 50% mutt), my elder sisters, Charlotte and Sandra, myself (Ron), and my younger brother, Charles (who has passed).

The home was very German. My dad, Reuben, had two ways to do things: his way and the wrong way.

He explained his view on the primary responsibility of parenting as preparing us for life after he and mother were gone. We were in our late teens at this time. He told us the way we would learn this was by the following scenario:

"At age twenty one, all life support from him would cease. No college tuition, no car support, no allowance and the requirement that we find our own place to live. We could come to visit for one to three days. Any laundry services would need to be pre-approved by Mom."

Sure enough at age twenty, I turned in my credit card, car keys, and found a place to live with two other guys.

Lesson: Raise your kids so that they can support themselves.

PS.: Both kids and their families would be welcome in our home if the need were to arise.

GROWING UP

LESSON BY MARY

PARENT RESPONSIBILITY - MARY

I was born and raised in a small town, Westby Wisconsin. I was the youngest in the family. My brother Owen was the "Brainiac" and my sister Jo Ann, was the "Beauty", and my brother Jim was good at all sports. My dad built and owned two movie theaters, owned an army surplus store, and tended a large garden. He was a WWI army vet. His growing up with a cruel stepmother instilled in him some undesirable qualities, but he also could be very funny.

My mother grew up on an Iowa farm where Norwegian was the language spoken. She was a sweet, steady presence in my life. Music was always playing on the phonograph, mostly the big bands and standards that my siblings chose. Dogs and cats were always in the family. I remember coal being delivered and my dad starting the furnace, on the cold mornings. He died suddenly when I was fourteen.

I think I was raised as much by my friends as my mom. Church was a big part of all our lives. My best friend Ardy and I were so close - sometimes we even dressed alike and people would refer to us as the Bobbsie twins. I am so thankful to have had such precious friends. These friendships have lasted to this day.

I attended St. Olaf college and loved my college experience. Right after graduation I was off on a Lutheran Exchange program to Denmark. There were 18 of us from all over, instant friends.

My first job was teaching in Fort Atkinson, Wis. I next went on to teach in St. Louis Park, Minnesota. Two friends had encouraged me to come to Minneapolis and share an apartment. That is where I met Ron.

Lesson: God can be real from an early age.

GROWING UP

LESSON

BE THERE FOR YOUR KID

I grew up in a family of six. Mom, Dad, two older sisters who taught me to dance, and a younger brother who was a better football player than I. And I was pretty good even with several knee reconstructions. We were a very competitive family with all of us involved in organized sports. Dad and mom were our best cheerleaders.

Even though Dad had his own business and worked long, long hours, he and mom came to every concert, play, or game. You always knew when he arrived at a game because his voice carried like a hand grenade that could penetrate thick walls. And since he knew how to improve our play, he always helped coach the game from the stands.

Lesson: Support your kid through your presence.

Psalm 127:3 Children are a gift from the LORD; they are a reward from him. NLT

GROWING UP

LESSON

BE WISE

Curfew, did not have one! I used to brag a lot about it at school especially before a big event when we expected to stay out really late.

What I did not tell them was how clever my dad was. He would come to me as I was going out the door and tell me to have a good time and to drive safely. Then he would remind me that it was Friday night and that he would be waking me up in the morning at five thirty to go to work with him.

I was usually home between ten and eleven o'clock

Lesson: Lots of ways to skin a cat. Look for the least painful.

Proverbs 22:6. Direct your children onto the right path, and when they are older, they will not leave it. NLT

GROWING UP

LESSON

ASSUMPTIONS

Dad was an entrepreneur. He founded the village of Mounds View, started a grocery store in our neighborhood, and founded Columbia and Capital Transit Company (a school bus company). It grew to be one of the largest in the five state area. It was the business I was planning to go into when I finished college. As such, with my future secured, I had a tendency to skip classes and enjoy college life. Then one afternoon I got a call from Dad telling me that he had sold the company. I went into shock, since he had done this without consulting me. I started to take school seriously again and go to class.

Lesson: Never assume even the "for sure" stuff.

Psalm 16:11. You will show me the way of life, granting me the joy of your presence and the pleasures of living with you forever. NLT

GROWING UP

LESSON

HELPING OUT WITH HOMEWORK

Mom was a really smart person. When she graduated from high school she taught grades one through eight in a small country school. Kids rode their horses to school and carried rifles to shoot rabbit and squirrels for the cooking pot at home.

I was in the ninth grade and taking Algebra One. Once Mr. Nelson, our teacher, when assigning homework for the weekend, told us that problem three was a very difficult problem and that there would be a prize for those who solved it correctly. I wanted that prize, so I asked Mom for her help. We puzzled over that problem for some time. The solution we came up with took up two pages of tablet paper. That Monday when Mr. Nelson asked who had solved the problem I raised my hand. I was the only one. Boy, were the buttons bursting on my shirt. Nelson asked if I would write my solution on the blackboard so the class could all see it. I did. It took some time as there were many lines of formula manipulation. Mr. Nelson upon seeing the solution was amazed. He awarded me the prize and also wrote an alternative solution on the board. His solution was about four lines as ours was about twenty lines.

Lesson: There can be many roads to a destination

James1:5. If you need wisdom, ask our generous God, and he will give it to you. He will not rebuke you for asking. NLT

GROWING UP

LESSON

MEDICAL

I "grew up" in Abbott Northwestern Hospital in downtown Minneapolis. I was born there, had a broken leg fixed there, tonsils removed there, several knee reconstructions there, and several heart treatments. The heart treatments included three electric conversions, and the installation of a pacemaker. Of the events, the broken leg was the most arduous.

When I was four or five years old, some friends and I were playing mumbly peg by the side of the road. It was a dirt road. A motorcyclist came down the road and lost control of his bike. The bike hit me breaking my right leg in three places. I was in a cast for nine months. I remember that the leg in the cast itched severely. I carried a butter knife with me all the time so I could reach under the cast with the blade and scratch. I also became proficient at walking on my hands, so much so that I could go up and down stairs on my hands.

Lesson: Kids shouldn't play in the street. Good thing God was watching over me.

GROWING UP

LESSON

COOKING

I love to cook. I started at an early age, I was under ten when I tried to bake my first creation, a Swedish tea ring. I know that my first effort in making the dough failed. I got rid of the faulty dough by tossing it out the dining room window. In doing this I left a trail of flour from the kitchen to the window. When Mom came home she of course followed the trail to the window and discovered the mess I had made outside. Have you ever tried cleaning up flour and dough from grass?

Lesson: Cooking errors are hard to hide from your mother.

Numbers 32:23. But if you fail to keep your word, then you will have sinned against the LORD, and you may be sure that your sin will find you out. NLT

GROWING UP

LESSON

FIRST KISS

I was a sophomore in high school, a good athlete, and dating a cheerleader, Jan. She was and is a great gal. In any event I was plotting my first kiss with her. This event was to take place at the end of the evening after a fall sock hop. We had double dated with a guy named, Charlie, who was a junior and had access to a car. The plan was simple. I walked Jan to the back door of her home as not to be visible from the street. Once there, I'd make my move. I made my move at the instant Jan's mom and dad drove into the backyard. We were highlighted in the headlights of their car.

I bolted. One of my athletic abilities was to reach full speed in two or three steps. The porch was wide enough such that I was going full speed when I ran into a wire clothesline chest high. I did a full three sixty landing on my back not able to breathe. Jan's mom came to the edge of the porch and inquired as to my condition. I croaked out that I was OK and I hurried to the car.

The next day I awoke with the world's largest hickey. My skin had been peeled off from chest high, up my neck, and under my chin. It was a tough few days in the locker room.

Lesson: God saved my life. If that wire had hit me in the throat instead of my chest I would have been a goner. Also, before taking off in the dark make sure there are no wires in front of you.

GROWING UP

LESSON

SLAPPING A WOMAN

I have struck a female, once. It was prom night our senior year in high-school. It was to be a big night. I had made reservations at a fancy restaurant some distance from our school, about a 45 minute drive. By the time we got there they had closed. So where to eat? The pressure mounted in the car and it was quite apparent my date and steady girlfriend for three years was not happy. (See first kiss) We ended up in a not so fancy part of St. Paul at an all night pizza joint. When we got back to the car Janet slapped me. I slapped her back. I wasn't happy with myself.

Lesson: It's true, don't hit a woman even if she strikes the first blow.

1 Peter 3:9. Don't repay evil for evil. Don't retaliate with insults when people insult you. Instead, pay them back with a blessing. That is what God has called you to do, and he will grant you his blessing. NLT

ATHLETICS

ATHLETICS

LESSON

TIMING IS EVERYTHING

I grew up in a very competitive family. Amongst ourselves it was board games like Monopoly or Scrabble. I also competed in football, basketball, and track. I suited up for varsity football from my freshman year. It was here that I injured my right knee for the first time, the year 1957. I re-injured it several times during my sophomore year and had my first knee surgery the following spring. Seven surgeries later, and twenty years later I had both knees replaced. Playing football, my longest run was seventy yards on a punt return in ninth grade. In the six years of playing as a running back, I never fumbled.

Lesson: Don't peak when playing a game in the ninth grade.

ATHLETICS

LESSON

DISCERNMENT

I was the shortest player on the basketball team at five feet eight inches. I was a very good defensive player. My strategy was simple. I would foul the person I was to guard hard……er, quite hard. It would make them twitchy. So all I had to do was touch them and they would flinch, usually missing their shot. Once I received a rebound under the opponent's basket. A quick glance at the clock said one second left so I shot the ball the entire court and made the shot. Bedlam ensued. Coach called time out and on the sidelined asked "What the hell were you doing"? He also pointed out that there was ten seconds left not one.

The next day I tried the same shot and could not get the ball to the basket.

Lesson: Make sure of what you are looking at before you act.

ATHLETICS

LESSON

WHO'S WILL

My first knee injury was my sophomore year in high school. It was at Hastings, Minnesota in the third quarter. We had had a pass intercepted and I had tried to tackle the runner and twisted my right knee. At this time, there was no knee reconstruction surgery. Needless to say, I re-injured that knee several more times during my high school years. I injured the left knee my sophomore year in college and subsequently injured that knee several times. Finally, after the fifth knee surgery, my doctor told me he was done operating on my knees, to quit playing football, and that, no matter what I was going to need both knees replaced in my early forties. He was right on all counts. I needed my knees replaced early forties and they wouldn't do it until my late fifties. That was twenty plus years ago.

Lesson: There is a time for gritty tenaciousness and a time to surrender to reality and God's will.

Proverbs 4:5. Get wisdom; develop good judgment.

ATHLETICS

LESSON

RUN THE RACE

After my short careers in organized team athletics, I turned to running and biking. I had built up to running five to seven miles a day, most every day. I have run in sixteen European countries, two South American, and in most every state in the United States. I then plotted a strategy to run my first marathon.

It was generally believed that a person could run three times his normal distance before his legs stopped. Since I ran seven miles a day I thought that if I got to twenty one miles that I was too stubborn to quit and could finish the 26 miles 385 yards on guts alone. So, in 1983 I signed up to run the Twin Cities (Minneapolis to St. Paul) Marathon. My sister Sandy and her daughter Karen decided to run with me to cheer me on.

Sandy hung with me for the first ten miles and then told me I was too slow (about nine minutes a mile) and that she was going to run her normal speed so she could finish. Karen hung with me. She gave up on me at about fifteen miles and started running her normal speed.

Alone at mile twenty-one there was a water station. I made the mistake of walking through the station. I could not get my legs to jog again and so planned to walk the last five miles. Sandy became concerned for me when I did not appear at the finish line, so she came out to find me. She did and immediately kicked my butt to get my legs going again so that I could finish.

Lesson: Run the race to completion. Just as the Apostle Paul exhorts us too.

ATHLETICS

LESSON

BICYCLES

After having to quit running (see knees) I turned to biking. Again, like all things, I was very type A about the ride. I rode in two RAGBRAI's (The Registries Annual Great Bike Ride Across Iowa), which is a seven day ride. I also rode in eleven TRAM's (The Ride Across Minnesota, which is a five day ride. These are tougher rides then you might think. You never realize how many steep hills there are in Iowa and Minnesota until you are riding a bike.

In one of the TRAMS I became dehydrated and went into atrial fibrillation. I felt terrible so I rode the sag wagon to the finish line for the day. I was at the first aid station hoping to feel better but did not. Finally, the attendant took my pulse. As he did I could see his face turn white. He thought I was having a heart attack. He put me in the ambulance and rushed me to the hospital. They discovered I was in A- Fib and immediately put me on a saline drip. During this my tent mate, Gene, came to see how I was doing. He showed proper concern for my health. But on his way out the door, he showed his other motivation. He asked, "What did you do with the beer money?

Lesson: If you are on an organized ride with other folks and are the keeper of the beer fund do drink enough water so you do not go into A-Fib and disappear with the beer fund.

[Remember, when it comes to life and death issues, beer comes in a close second.]

MARRIAGE, LIFE AND PARENTHOOD

MARRIAGE, LIFE AND PARENTHOOD

LESSON

MOVES

In the early 60's I lived in an apartment on Pillsbury Ave in Minneapolis Minnesota. In the apartment right above us were three single teachers. I cleverly thought that a good way to meet them was to give them a call and see if anyone would like to learn how to play chess. The cutest of the lot was named Mary. She said she would. So, after two or three sessions of chess, I asked if she would like to go out dancing and have a beer. Being from Wisconsin she answered she would like to go out for a beer. It turned out she was also a good dancer.

In any event, on this first date I told her that I thought we would get married. After all, she was of the same political persuasion as I, and she was a Christian like me. And she laughed at my jokes. This caused an eye roll. After the next dance, I told her that if she "would marry me I would show her the world." This brought an eye roll and a chortle. This date was in early December, 1962. That March, 1963 we were engaged to be married and did get married that July. Together for 58 years, so far.

Lesson: Don't promise someone something because God is listening and may deliver on the promise.

MARRIAGE, LIFE AND PARENTHOOD

LESSON

BLUE EARTH, MINNESOTA (Part 1)

We moved to Blue Earth in December 1965. Winter in Minnesota is cold, very cold. The moving van unloaded in the late afternoon into the early evening, with the doors propped open. It was late that night by the time we got a bed put together. We had rented the lower level of a big old home in almost downtown Blue Earth. As we were getting ready for bed we noticed that the house was very, very cold. It would not warm up. The next day we discovered that the storm windows had not been put on. At that time, you used screen windows in the summer and in the fall swap out the screen windows for an extra set of glass windows called, storm windows. Putting on the storm windows and finding the electric blanket solved our cold problem.

Lesson: If you move in December to Minnesota make sure the house has its storm windows on and unpack the electric blanket first!

Psalm 57:10. For your unfailing love is as high as the heavens. Your faithfulness reaches to the clouds. NLT

MARRIAGE, LIFE AND PARENTHOOD

LESSON

BLUE EARTH, MINNESOTA (Part 2)

While living in Blue Earth I traveled a great deal. I was usually gone two or three nights a week. One time on coming home Mary complained that a bathroom toilet in the back hall was running. It was a seldom used toilet. I checked the water tank and saw that it was not running. I did not raise the lid to check the toilet bowl.

I left again the next day. Mary continued to hear noise from that toilet. She went to check the toilet tank and found that it was not running. SHE THEN RAISED THE LID AND CHECKED THE BOWL. There in the bowl was a large sewer rat which had come up the dried trap and into the bowl. Slamming the lid she went to seek aid. It came in the form of Arnie, our next door neighbor, with heavy leather gloves and a club. He took care of it.

Lesson: If possible, live next door to a fearless neighbor.

Proverbs 27:10. Never abandon a friend— either yours or your father's. When disaster strikes, you won't have to ask your brother for assistance. It's better to go to a neighbor than to a brother who lives far away. NLT

MARRIAGE, LIFE AND PARENTHOOD

LESSON

BLUE EARTH, MINNESOTA (Part 3)

CHANGING THE BABY

Our son, Ian was born in Blue Earth, Minnesota on December 3, 1965. He was our first born and as such a great learning experience. He did not come with a "How To" manual. Mary's mom Louise came to help out for the first few days when baby and Mary came home. Since I traveled a lot, I missed the first few days of Ian being home. In any event, when I came home, I was greeted with loud hoots and shouts of dismay from Mary and Louise. When I looked into the room, I saw Ian on his back on the changing table with urine spouting into the air like Old Faithful at Yellowstone Park.

Lesson: Cold air will often cause little boys to urinate, cover the urinator.

MARRIAGE, LIFE AND PARENTHOOD

LESSON

ST. PAUL/UNIVERSITY OF MINN HOUSING

After three years of working in Blue Earth, Sinclair Oil was kind enough to give us time off so I could finish course work for my undergraduate degree. I needed fifteen credits of a foreign language with a "C" average to graduate. I went to two summer sessions and received grades of "C" and "B". Ten credits of Spanish above a "C" average. All I did that summer was take Spanish, study Spanish and talk Spanish. It was Spanish, Spanish, Spanish all summer, same teacher, same text book. In the fall, I switched to a night session. DISASTER STRUCK. Different professor and a different textbook. I was completely lost and had failed the mid-term test. I then did something that all red blooded American males would do…I cried. I related to the professor my plight. I needed a "D" to get my degree. Taking the final test, I knew I had failed. The professor gave me a "D". I got the degree.

Lesson: Tears work with a college professor, even if you're a guy.

IRONY: Both of our children became fluent in the Spanish language.

James 1:12. God blesses those who patiently endure testing and temptation. Afterward they will receive the crown of life that God has promised to those who love him. NLT

MARRIAGE, LIFE AND PARENTHOOD

LESSON

LOS ANGELES

We had just moved to Fountain Valley, CA in Orange County to a small townhome. We had rented it with a portion of the rent going towards a down payment. It was our intent to buy it. As such Mary decided that improvements needed to be made. Such as wall papering the first level powder room. Being small, I thought the job would go quick and easy to do. It was not easy. Getting the paper to fit around sink, toilet, towel racks, cabinets, and door frames was a major pain in the butt. To do the job took an entire day and three extra trips to the wall paper store for advice. (There is a lesson here.). At the end of the day looking at the room I was quite proud of myself. It looked pretty good.

That night we were awakened in the early morning hours by a very strange noise of paper being torn up. I was frightened at first to go downstairs to see what was wrecking our downstairs area. Then I realized that the noise was the wall paper in the powder room rolling back. The noise was the paper coming off the walls. Checking it in the morning proved that this was true. The paper in the room had come off the walls and had rolled up in perfect rolls stuck to random spots on the bathroom walls.

Lesson: Leave it to the pros.

MARRIAGE, LIFE AND PARENTHOOD

LESSON BY MARY

WILLIES WORLD

In 1984 we took in a stray pregnant cat and arranged a birthing room in a downstairs closet. Soon her litter of five was born. Noticing a white ball of fluff with one green eye and one blue eye, we decided this was the one to keep. The remaining kittens were quickly adopted. We named our little beauty Lilly. Time passed and it was time for her spaying. The vet informed us that Lilly was a Willy and should be brought back in a couple of weeks for castration. So, Lilly became Willy.

Years later we planned a major remodel of our house. As soon as our builder started and chaos reigned, Willy left. Oh the sadness, as he was a great cat. We moved to an apartment as the house was unlivable. When we came back to the house six weeks later, we continued to call out for Willy. One afternoon Ron was sitting on the deck and called me to come quickly. Here comes Willy trotting up from the lakeshore over a hill of dirt. Such joy. The lost came home.

Lesson: Our God answers prayers even when hope seems lost.

Luke 15:24. For this son of mine was dead and has now returned to life. He was lost, but now he is found.' So the party began. NLT

CATS WE HAVE KNOWN

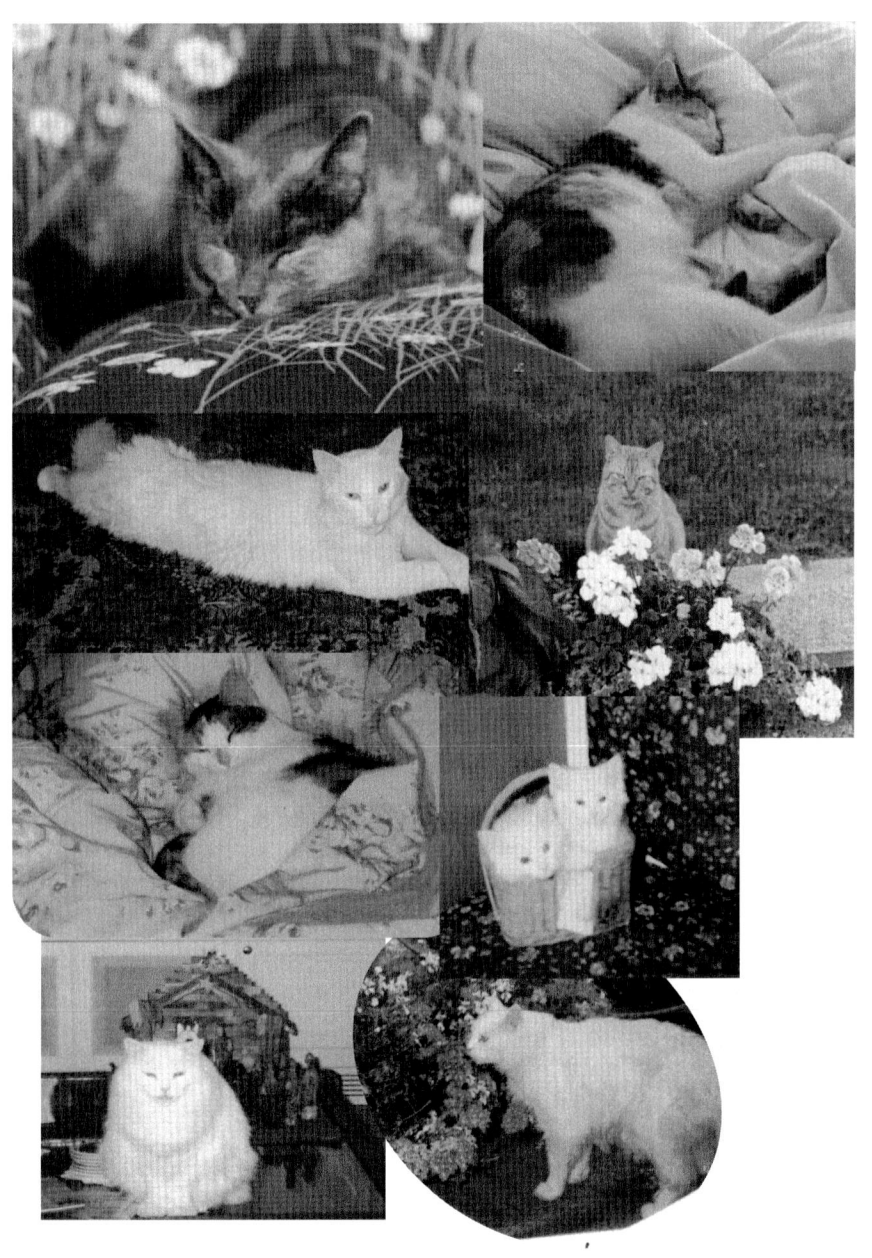

MARRIAGE, LIFE AND PARENTHOOD

LESSON

PROTECTION FOR YOUR KID

Our daughter Amy and her husband, Mike, moved to Costa Rica and bought three acres of jungle property overlooking the Gulf of Mexico. They hacked out of this jungle, a site for their home. This was not our idea of a safe spot to live, so I was in constant prayer that the Lord send angels to guard the kids.

On our first visit, we were relieved to see that Amy and Mike had adopted two dogs. Kaya, a huge dog, was a cross of a Doberman Pincher and a Great Dane. She was Great Dane in size, and when this dog barked the whole village came to a halt. Kaya was very protective. And Bear, was a very friendly black lab. They went everywhere that Amy went.

Lesson: Angels come in many forms.

MARRIAGE, LIFE AND PARENTHOOD

LESSON

ENTERTAINMENT

Mary and I had been living in Brussels, Belgium and had come back to Minnesota on home leave. We were staying with Mom and Dad. The kids were in the third and fifth grades of school. They related that it would be great if my dad, their grandfather, would take them to see Steve Martin at the State Fair. He did.

Martin comes out to great applause. The first words out of his mouth are "Have you ever wondered what happens to a fart? Well since it is hot air it rises in the air till it reaches a layer above air level. This layer is the fart layer." Well the kids are rolling in the aisles while dad is trying not to laugh while showing his disagreement with the topic.

Lesson: Stand-up comics tend not to be "G" rated at live shows.

MARRIAGE, LIFE AND PARENTHOOD

LESSON

TEMPER

While I was growing up I was known to have a temper and since I could do a 1000 pushups and was built like a brick out house, I took no prisoners.

Living overseas we would come home once a year for two weeks of what was called home leave. The family and I were out shopping for American stuff. We had exited 35W going south at County Road 42. I must have cut this guy off for I heard some irritated horn honks. Looking in the rearview I noticed nothing special about the car. He exited the highway with us and proceeded to follow us into the Burnsville Mall parking lot. I went up and down a couple of rows to confirm that he was following us. When going down a row I slammed on the brakes, hopped out of my car, and jogged back to his now stopped car. Reaching through the open window I grabbed a handful of the guy's shirt and yanked him halfway out of his window. I then explained to him how many bones I would break if he didn't stop this nonsense. He stopped. When I got back in our own car Mary and the kids were on the floor of the car.

Through prayer and The Good Lord my temper has greatly improved.

Lesson: Prayer works. Today I would probably be shot.

Proverbs 14:29. People with understanding control their anger; a hot temper shows great foolishness. NLT

MARRIAGE, LIFE AND PARENTHOOD

LESSON

ACCIDENTS

Our son Ian was home for the weekend from college. It was a snowy and sleeting type day in Minnesota. He picked up his sister Amy, a high school junior, as they had a lunch date with their dad in Bloomington. Ian drove an older Land Cruiser. Driving home after the lunch on 35E they were following a state of Minnesota plow truck which was spreading salt and sand on the road bed. The truck was going slowly so Ian passed the truck. When returning to his lane he lost control of the truck because of the ice. It rolled over two and one-half times ending up on its roof. As it rolled Ian kept asking, "Amy, are you OK?" Thankfully both were buckled in.

Minutes later Ron drove by and saw the commotion and Ian's truck down in the ravine on its roof. He stopped on the road in front of a state trooper's car. Ron spotted the two kids waving at him from the rear seat of the trooper's car. Joy and relief!!

Lesson: The road in front of a plow truck laying down salt and sand is icy and dangerous.

Amy and Ian

Proverbs 14:26. Those who fear the LORD are secure; he will be a refuge for their children.

49

MARRIAGE, LIFE AND PARENTHOOD

LESSON

HANDYMAN

Some people have the "fix-it" gene. I do not. I call outside help to change light bulbs. Once it took me a month to change a single bulb. When I was actively working, I would many times be home only for the weekend. One Friday night upon getting home Mary told me that the hall light was burned out. I told her I would look at it Saturday morning. The next day when taking the burnt bulb out I saw that the bulb had fused to the fixture in burning out. NO way that bulb was coming out of the bulb fixture. So I cut the now useless bulb and fixture wires to remove it. Now I had bare wires and no light fixture for the hallway. Trip One was to a hardware store for new fixture hardware. Once there, I realized that I do not know how to reconnect wiring. I gave up for the weekend. Next weekend comes. Trip two to the hardware store and I get an explanation on how to reconnect wires. I reconnect wires and reassemble fixture. Flip wall switch and … … no light. Take fixture apart, let parts rest on table till following weekend. Next weekend comes. Trip three to hardware store, take parts with, ask hardware guy how to put together. He does it, leaving me the simple task of connecting four wires. I could do that! There is light. Three weeks to change the bulb

Lesson: God has gifted some people the ability to fix stuff. Not me.

MARRIAGE, LIFE, AND PARENTHOOD

LESSON

FRIENDSHIP AND TENACITY

We had prayed for two years about the building of downtown Burnsville and were sure it was something God wanted me to do. I am still sure. Mary, my bride of 45 years was not so sure. She was sure when she saw the first shovel of dirt come out of the ground. I was determined to have a catering business there. I did and it was called The International Chef's Culinary Center. It was a catering business able to feed 450 people at a time. All business P&L's (profit and loss report) have a set of business ratios that they must operate within to be profitable. I did not have the correct set of ratios. My rent was too high and the landlord would not re-negotiate the rent. We went broke. So, one day after 55 years of marriage, I came home and told Mary we have $10 left. She, to her credit did not scream too loudly, but more importantly she stayed with me. She kept her wedding oath and stuck with me during this tough time.

Lesson: The people who stick with you during tough times demonstrate true love.

MARRIAGE, LIFE, AND PARENTHOOD

LESSON

WORRY

Let's talk worry. I either created or read the 90-5-5 rule of worry. This rule is that 90% of the stuff you worry about does not happen, 5% you have no control over, and 5% you can work with. Recently I was diagnosed with a pinched nerve in my lower back. The doc's recommended a steroid shot to ease the pain. To do this I would have to stop taking a blood thinner called Warfarin. I am in A-Fib all the time. This drug thins the blood so that it won't clot. I am dependent on this drug. (It's rat poison, by the way.) To do this, you bridge the gap with a drug called Enoxaparin. (Spelling of drugs is optional on my part). The Enoxaparin requires a shot in the stomach every twelve hours. I could not imagine sticking a needle into my stomach every twelve hours. So I got everybody I knew involved in looking for someone who could give me the shots. I mean everybody. Couldn't find anyone. So if I was going to get the spinal, I would have to give myself the shot. I decided I had to. So several nights ago I was ready to give myself the first shot, at three AM. I couldn't believe it, there was no pain, the needle is so sharp you do not feel it go in. I got the injection. The hardest part was laying on my stomach for ten minutes. Which could be another story.

Lesson: 90% of the stuff you worry about does not happen.

Luke 12:25. Can all your worries add a single moment to your life? NLT

MARRIAGE, LIFE, AND PARENTHOOD

LESSON

MALE MENOPAUSE

All men go through male menopause. This usually happens during his forties, but it is when he figures out that he is not going to be king. He then does one of three things. (I reserve the right to be wrong here but I am close to the truth if not on it.). He buys a red sports car, or starts to date a twenty year old bimbo and ruins his family life, or turns to cooking. I skipped the red sports car, and bimbo and turned to cooking at age 8. Still cooking and happily married.

Lesson: One king in your life is enough, Jesus.

Revelations 19:16. On his robe at his thigh was written this title: King of all kings and Lord of all lords. NLT

MARRIAGE, LIFE, AND PARENTHOOD

LESSON

YOU EAT WITH YOUR EYES FIRST

When you bake you need to follow the recipe as the successful product is dependent on the interaction of the ingredients in the making of the batter and the baking of the batter.   I was going to make a chocolate torte recipe out of "Baking by Chocolate".   It looked great on the cover of the magazine.   An important note here was that I was under heavy pressure from a consulting and treasured baker named Mary to use a Brownie Mix.   Being a purist I made it from scratch.   I also decided to make it when the treasured baker was not home.

Well, I made the batter, and preheated the oven, I noted that it called for a nine inch round pan and when I put the batter in it, it filled the pan to the top.   This was bad as things tend to expand when heated.   I double and tripled check the pan size against the recipe.   Having done this I put the pan in the oven to bake.   I happened to walk by the oven about twenty minutes later and noted shooting flames in the oven.   First mistake: I opened the oven door to put out the fire.   Second mistake: I forgot that the smoke and fire alarm in our house was linked to the Burnsville Fire Department.   When I opened the door the alarm went off.   I opened the front door and back doors to let the smoke out. As I was contemplating the disaster in the oven I noted a presence standing next to me. It was a friend from church who was a captain in the Burnsville Fire department.   He questioned as to how my baking was going, then he laughed.   The cake had fallen in the center leaving a crater in the middle of the cake.

I needed to slice the cake horizontally to put ganache between the layers.   When I did this I had a huge hole into the middle of the cake.   I filled the hole with chocolate ganache.   When done it looked exactly like the picture on the front cover of the magazine. A chocolate torte decorated with sliced pecans.   It was beautiful.   I told the treasured baker my plan was to take it to work the next day and she was not to try any of it.   Well the next day I noted that someone had eaten at least two pieces from the cake.

I took the cake to the office and put it in the pantry in slices. It was gone in less than five minutes.

Lesson: People eat with their eyes first and if you cover your mistake with chocolate frosting you get a highly complimented dessert.

MARRIAGE, LIFE AND PARENTHOOD

LESSON

THE SNOOPY STORY

The only dog we had was acquired in Brussels, Belgium. We lived in Rhode St. Genese, Belgium. Soon after moving there Ian and Amy discovered a farm close by and up a hill. They along with neighborhood kids were making daily treks up the hill to visit the pups at the farm. The runt of the litter became their favorite and they often brought him home with them. Seeing he was flea infested we purchased a flea collar, but when the farmer noticed this he would remove the collar and put it on another more favored pup. Many flea collars were bought until I'm sure all the farm dogs were "collared". Ian and Amy pleaded with their dad to keep the pup and finally Ron walked up the hill to ask if we could keep him. The farmer agreed for a rather hefty price.

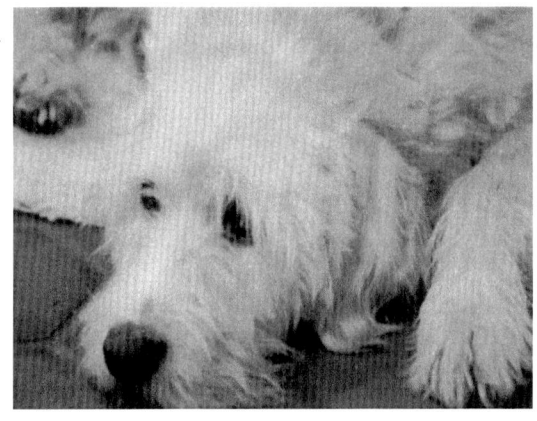

So this Belgium farm dog became ours, giving rise to more disagreements. Ron did not want him in the house (1st. Stage), then Snoopy was to stay in the kitchen (2nd Stage), and at last he had the run of the house and was soon sleeping with the kids at night.

Ron still wanting an outside dog, contacted a carpenter who didn't understand English to build a doghouse. Ron's arm motions as measurements were misinterpreted. Well, Snoopy got his "petit maison." It would have been roomy for a Great Dane! Our two kids, plus the neighborhood kids, could all fit in there with Snoopy. Cozy with straw and

56

rags on the floor, the kids all thought it was great. Snoopy not so much - he only wanted to be where his people lived.

Lesson: Child/dog love is irrepressible.

Psalm 36:6. You care for people and animals alike, O LORD. NLT.

Wedding Day

Early On

Later On

Ian and Christine
Wedding Day

Ian and Christine
Later On

Ian and Christine and Kids

Amy and Michael
Wedding Day

Amy and Michael
Later On

Amy and Michael and Kids

Family Time with Kids and Grandkids

INTERNATIONAL LIVING

INTERNATIONAL LIVING

LESSONS

SEE STUFF

We have lived on four of the seven continents and visited a fifth continent a lot. We stood on the Great Wall of China, prayed at the Wailing Wall in Jerusalem, climbed over Hadron's Wall in England, and had the cold water at Wall Drug in South Dakota.

Great Wall of China

We have visited:

Battle of Waterloo Monument
Seen The David in Florence, Italy (A must see)
Seen The Mona Lisa (Great disappointment)
The Beach at Normandy
The pyramids of Egypt
The Sphinx
The Beach of Ipanema
Machu Picchu in Peru
The Forbidden City of China
The Great Wall of China
Civil War battle grounds

Lesson: God's Wonders are everywhere!

INTERNATIONAL LIVING

LESSON

LIVING IN COUNTY SURREY AREA (LONDON)

Willow Cottage Virginia Water

Looking Good in London

Ladies Day at Ascot

**LaBurnham Cottage
Engelfield Green**

INTERNATIONAL LIVING

LESSON

BRUSSELS, BELGIUM

Mary and I arrived in Brussels and were just settled in our hotel. It was our visit to find a home to live in. My "bride" Mary was with me. Since it was around 6:00 pm I thought I would give my boss a call and see if he and his wife could join us for dinner. The maid answered speaking French. I did recognize my boss's last name mentioned in her greeting so I knew I had the correct number. Of course, I did not understand a word she said. So I said goodbye and dug out my "Speaking French" book and figured out how to ask If Manny was home. Manny was my boss. So armed with how to ask if

Manny was home in French, I called back and asked for Manny in French. How clever of me, of course she answered in French of which I did not understand one word she said. She then tried Flemish, same thing no understanding. Then German, no understanding. Then Spanish. Since Mary did speak a little Spanish we were able to establish that he was not home and she did not know when he would be home.

Lesson: The average Belgian speaks on average three languages while the undereducated American speaks one and poorly.

1 Peter 4:11. Do you have the gift of speaking? Then speak as though God himself were speaking through you. NLT

INTERNATIONAL LIVING

LESSON

PARIS. FRANCE

I was visiting our subsidiary in France for a sales review of our product line. Having time before the review I checked into my hotel and took my things up to my room. After hanging clothes up, I decided to take a short rest before the arduous review. Since I did not want to wrinkle my suit pants I took them off and was resting in my underwear. God has gifted me with the ability to go to sleep at any time of the day in about 60 seconds. I was sound asleep when awakened by a clutch of young Japanese females. They came into my room with lots of giggling, lots of screaming, and whoops, whoops whooping. Apparently, the hotel clerk had given them the wrong room key. Both they and I were surprised.

Lesson: When in a hotel resting, throw the manual door lock to make sure that no one can get in.

INTERNATIONAL LIVING

LESSON

MILAN, ITALY

Most cities in the world have an identity, a reason for being there. Milan Italy is known for its leather goods. In Europe men carry man purses which carry your passport, different country currencies, and other guy stuff. I was in need of a new bag. So, on my first trip to Milan, I was anxious to get out and do some shopping. So, I was in the main shopping district window shopping men's bags. (You know how it is when someone has come into your space?). All of sudden I felt someone invade my space. I turned to confront them and found myself face to face with a very beautiful woman. I, of course, asked how I could help her. She told me in very clear English how I could help and how much it would cost in dollars. I did not know I could run that fast in a suit on a summer day.

Lesson: Be careful of the people you ask, "How can I help?". They might tell you.

Proverbs 5:15. Drink water from your own well, share your love only with your wife. NLT

INTERNATIONAL LIVING

LESSON

BRUSSELS, BELGIUM

I am reminded of our first Thanksgiving celebration in Brussels of 1976. Turkeys were not to be found in the markets. A fellow expatriate suggested I try a special order from my local butcher. So the expensive order was made. We were going to have our traditional Thanksgiving.

As the day came and the bird was roasting the aromas were telling us that something was amiss. Well, when the turkey was done maybe it would taste just fine. But as we gathered to feast one taste of the turkey proved there would not be a second. It tasted like fish - how could a turkey become fish?

The dog and the cat didn't mind it.

I confronted the butcher the next day and he confessed that the bird had been fed fish meal to plump it up. And no, there was no refund

Lesson: Do not mess with American tradition in another country.

INTERNATIONAL LIVING

LESSON

BRUSSELS BELGIUM

Early on while living in Brussels, I noticed that many public places had only one restroom for use by both genders. Also in parks, urinals were attached to the outside walls of the restroom buildings, and guys would be doing their business in the wide open spaces.

This hit home early as I was in the men's room at our office doing my business. I was at the urinal when the cleaning lady walked in without so much as a "Hello, cleaning lady coming in!". She started cleaning the urinal next to me as I was completing my task. She wasn't embarrassed even a little bit. Surprisingly neither was I.

Lesson: Toilet rules are different in different countries.

INTERNATIONAL LIVING

LESSON

SOUTH AMERICA

Living in Caracas Venezuela brought many adventures and learning moments. An early on experience was when we moved into our very expensive penthouse. The city sits at about five thousand feet and pumped its water supply up from sea level. Terrorists blew up two of the three pumps. Therefore, our very expensive penthouse had no water. The building had a water reserve of 11,000 liters. So twice a day at 6:00 am and 4:00 pm the water would come on for fifteen minutes. During this time you would refill your tub, run your wash machine, flush toilets, water plants, and maybe take a shower in cold water. If you were visiting friends in the building at the time water came on, you could hear the pipes began to rattle. We would make a bee line back to our place to do all the jobs that needed water.

Lesson: When you turn on a faucet, water doesn't necessarily come out.

James 5:8. You, too, must be patient. Take courage, for the coming of the Lord is near.

INTERNATIONAL LIVING

LESSON BY MARY

PERU

In a final hurrah trip we decided to visit Machu Picchu, in Peru. We flew from Caracas to Lima, Peru and then to the colonial town of Cuzco, steeped in history. Upon departing the plane in Cuzco we were given a cup of cocoa tea to alleviate high altitude symptoms. Didn't work for our son, Ian. Leaving him at the hotel the three of us went to explore this fascinating town and its large cathedral in town center. Ron thought the town smelled like the restroom in a small bar in Northern Minnesota that badly needed cleaning.

The next morning the four of us boarded a train to take us to the foot of Machu Picchu. From there a bus took us on a winding road up the mountain, pure amazement and fear on Ron's part. We checked into a small inn where I think we were the only lodgers for the night. What the Incas built was an incredible feat of engineering, the enormous stones fit together with precision. We had a full day of wandering the phenomenal ruins. Also, we noted the long footpath behind the town. It was the escape path from the invading Spaniards.

We arose early the next morning so as to not miss a Machu Picchu sunrise. I remember Amy and I watching as the sun crept into view.

We were awestruck at experiencing such beauty and the complete silence. Just our family was there to share the moment. "How Great Thou Art" came to us and we sang.

Lesson: God has left us with lots of stuff to see how great He is. Make memories!

Psalm 104:1. O LORD my God, how great you are! You are robed with honor and majesty.

INTERNATIONAL LIVING

LESSON BY MARY

CHINA

Since Ron was working in China he thought I should make the trip to see if I would care to move there. So the flight was booked. I was feeling some stress with such a long flight and no husband to hold my hand. My eyes were irritated from the moment I awoke the morning of the flight. I have a condition: Shogren's Syndrome that's related to my Lupus. Its main condition is dry eyes.

Looking Good in Bejing

On the plane, I became terribly distressed with my sore eyes and the long flight became a nightmare of pain. I was blinded and miserable – barely able to open my eyes.

God gave me an angel of a seatmate who was very caring. She asked the flight attendant to guide me when we arrived at the Narita Airport in Japan for a two hour layover. She brought me to the lounge and left me until the flight to Beijing. Then she led me to the plane and my seat. My second angel sent by God.

I was so helpless and I couldn't move without her help. Arriving in Beijing, another hurdle was filling out the paperwork to go through customs. Again a flight attendant came to the rescue. I was then on my own, baggage in hand and out the gate where Ron would spot me.

But, many minutes passed and I was feeling alone and desperate and still mostly blind. Finally Chin, Ron's driver, spotted me and I was at last rescued. Ron was there with flowers of welcome.

Lesson: God's angels will be there for the helpless and lost.

Psalm 91:11 For he will order his angels to protect you wherever you go.

INTERNATIONAL LIVING

LESSON

BRUSSELS BELGIUM

MOWING THE GRASS

It rains about 200 days per year in Brussels. That means that on a day it doesn't rain you mow the grass. In moving to Belgium we bought a new mower to take with us. So on the first day that the sun was shining, the grass was long, and since we were expecting company, I decided to mow. This was about seven AM.

I got out the new mower, still in the box, and noted that the box had the world's three ugliest words. "Some Assembly Required". Put it together and found that it would not start.

House and yard in Brussels.

Got the manual out and carefully read the manual part where it told you what to do if the mower would not start. Followed the instructions, mower would not start.

My son Ian, who was 11 at the time, was a good manual instruction follower. He went through the steps and discovered that the manual was not the correct manual for the mower. Made me angry. About ten AM now.

I call a friend and ask if he was done mowing his lawn and, if so, could I borrow his? He was, so I hopped in the car and went down to Waterloo, yep where Napoleon met his, and picked up Al's mower.

So around 11:00 AM I start to mow our lawn. I do not notice but I am mowing so that the mowed grass is being thrown out onto the unmowed part that as I mow, the grass is getting thicker. The grass is wet so it wasn't too long before the mower clogged and choked on the plugged grass and stopped. I saw my error, unplug the mower from clogged grass, and prepare to restart the mower. So I pull on the rope, it breaks. I am now irritated.

Have you ever disassembled a lawn mower's rope pull assembly? When you take off the cover you note that there is a tightly wound spring that returns the rope. Scared me, for I knew, if I sprung that spring then I was in deep doodoo! I had.

Aides in the grass cutting.

It is now about 3:00 PM and I am now officially livid. I decide to throw money at it. I get Amy, who is about nine, but has better French than I, and go to the local equivalent of Target. With her we get a mower that has an English manual. I feel a little better now, even though I am on my third lawn mower that day. The box also has the three ugly words.

We get the box home and I start the assembly. It is going great until I get to the grass bag that attaches to the mower. Somehow they had sown the channel for the support rods closed. The rod would not go through. It is now about five PM. Company due at six. So I call Al and tell him about his broken mower rope and ask if he could come early and try to put the new one together. He gets to our house, I give him a large gin and tonic, the mower bag, and the rods that needed to be threaded through the bag. Put him in a room and told him not to come out until the bag was assembled. Soon Al pokes his head out the door and tells me the bag channels have been sown shut. I tell him I know, and that he would not get out of that room until he had the bag together. About an hour later out he comes.

81

I am finishing the mowing after six and company arrival. It took about twelve hours to mow lawn not much larger than a postage stamp.

Lesson: Sometimes the simplest task can become difficult.

INTERNATIONAL LIVING

LESSON

BRUSSELS BELGIUM

WATER DAMAGE

We were going skiing in the Alps. We would be gone for five days so we had two teenage girls from the American community staying at the house. The house was three stories. Lots of marble, including two marble staircases.

Upon our return I noticed that there was water in the garage. Going up the first staircase, I noted a river of water running down the stairs from the first floor.

I was filled with dread as I feared I would find two teenage girls murdered and stuffed into tubs of running water. When I reached the first floor we noted that the water was cascading down the staircase. Visions of what I would find upstairs got worse. With trepidation I ascended the next staircase.

Upon reaching the third floor I discover no bodies and a fill pipe that had pulled out from a toilet, and was shooting water out like a running faucet. I get the water turned off.

A note from the girls indicated the time that they had left. If the pipe had burst right after the girls left, then it was running for a maximum of six hours. In that time the kitchen ceiling was ruined, rugs were soaked, and the pool table had to be bailed out. Thousands of dollars of damage were done. Took months to complete repairs.

Lesson: When you leave your house, turn the water off.

83

SALES

SALES

LESSON

ALL YOU NEED TO KNOW ABOUT SALES

A top performing sales person will have the following qualities and traits in priority order:

Tenacity

Street Smarts

Ability to Plan and Execute to it

Product Knowledge

Territory Knowledge

That they conduct themselves legally, morally, and ethically.

When negotiating deals a sales person should always have in his back pocket the "I can't do that, my boss would have to answer that". If needed, use the sales technique of "Call the higher power card" no matter what your level is.

Lesson: Hire people with these qualities and who are smarter than yourself, and fear The Lord.

SALES

LESSON

HOTELS AND MOTELS RULES

In my sales career I had three jobs, Sinclair Oil (retail rep), Control Data (sales rep and manager), and Fourth Shift (Sales Executive). All required extensive travel, locally throughout the US and then internationally to Europe, South America, and the Far East. My real life experience helped me create a set of "traveler" rules, all based on the same corner stone: FAMILIARITY.

My first serious job was as a sales representative for Sinclair Oil, my territory was Southern Minnesota. As such, I was gone many weeks from Monday to Thursday as I traveled the territory by company car. I stayed in many one story highway motels located in the small towns of Southern Minnesota. They all had one thing in common. The showers were too small as was the soap bar and bath towels. The towels were about the size of a large washcloth. When showering I would often lose the bar of soap in one of my skin folds instituting a search.

RULE ONE: STAY IN ONE BRAND OF HOTEL THAT USE NORMAL SIZE BARS OF SOAP AND THE TOWELS ARE OF NORMAL SIZE. MARRIOTT

Later in my sales career my travels required the rental of a car. At the time, I drove GM Cadillac cars. Early on I rented a Toyota (something) on a dark and stormy night. The courtesy dropped me off in a downpour. First, I could not find the key hole in the dark and second, when the key hole was found, I searched for the correct key to use. I got soaked!

RULE TWO: RENT THE SAME CAR AS YOU DRIVE AT HOME.

Lesson: When traveling, continuity and familiarity are important

SALES

LESSON

SMART PEOPLE

My dad taught me a lot of stuff. He was an entrepreneur and very innovative person. He taught that if I were to hire people that I should always hire people smarter than yourself. Harder to manage but would make business life a lot easier. I took this advice. When hiring sales people for our software company I would always test them. I had taken the same battery of tests. If they did not score better than I, I did not hire them.

Doing this I had five of the best sales people I have had the pleasure of working with. They made a lot of money and set a strong base of sales for our fledgling company. Their success created one problem. I did have to widen the doors at work so they and their egos could get through. And conducting a sales meeting was managing a cat fight.

Lesson: A little pain can mean large gains

Psalm 101:6. I will search for faithful people to be my companions.

SALES

LESSON

VALUE OF A SECOND

I learned early in my sales career the true meaning of the old saying that time is money. I sold computer time usage contracts for Control Data. There were levels of priority that the computer would look for jobs based on the rate per second you were paying. Priorities were set from priority one through priority six. The fastest processing was level six which cost $1,200.00 per second. The computer was capable of doing millions of instructions per second. The Control Data 6600 was the world's fastest computer at the time. It helped design the Boeing 747 and the Saturn rocket. People who understood a computer and what it could do in a second knew the $1,200.00 to be a fair price.

Lesson: What you do with your time has value.

SALES

LESSON

EAVESDROPPING

My first sales territory with Control Data was Orange County California. There are a lot of aerospace and defense contractors in this county. One of my early on prospects was Hughes Aircraft in Fullerton. I was on my way to a 1:30 pm meeting at Hughes and thought I would catch a quick bite at a Coco's Restaurant. I happen to hear a couple of guys talking about Hughes Aircraft. My ears perked up. Turns out the two guys were my competitors for the Hughes project. These were the "hated Univac guys." They were discussing pricing and other sales strategy for the deal. Of course, I took notes in great detail. Based on these notes, I won the deal. I am guessing that the Univac guys never knew why they lost the deal,

Lesson: Savvy salespeople, NEVER, NEVER, NEVER discuss a deal in public, using real names and numbers.

SALES

LESSON

SALES MANAGEMENT 101

My first Sales management job was as Branch Manager of Time Sharing sales (for computer usage) in Boston Ma. My best salesman was a guy named Ken. His office and desk area was a mess and did not meet corporate guidelines for neatness. This was overlooked because Ken was the top sales guy in the office.

Well, Ken went on vacation and I decided to clean up his office. With the help of my office admin we did just that. Where there were stacks of paper now was a clean desktop. I thought Ken would really be pleased. I was in my office the following Monday when Ken returned. My first clue that something was wrong was when I heard him scream. He knew where everything was before with the disorder, but now he couldn't find anything since we had filed it all. It took him two weeks of very valuable time to find all his stuff.

Lesson: If it ain't broke don't fix it.

SALES

LESSON

PROMOTION INTERVIEWS: CLOSING A DEAL

After being a sales manager in Boston, a promotion opportunity became available in Minneapolis. It was a key slot that all had to pass to become upper level managers. It was as a staff aide to an Executive Vice President (EVP) of marketing and sales for a major geography of the world. The open position was staff aide to EVP of Eastern US, Manny Otis. I flew from Boston to Minneapolis for the interview. I had cleverly arranged it so I would be the last interview. (This could be a law in any sales cycle. Always be last to present.). My interview was on a Friday. I thought the interview went well. My competition was a guy who had the same position as I but in New York City. After the interview, Manny told me that he would call Monday or Tuesday and let me know my status. On leaving I noticed a smaller office next to Manny's that was empty. It would be the new guy's office. So instead of going back to Boston I stayed the week end and on Monday early morning, I occupied the office. A little later Manny came in, saw me in the office and asked what I was doing. I answered that since I thought he was going to give me the job, I would show up for work early. This closed the deal.

Lesson: Physical presence at the right time is of prime importance.

SALES

LESSON

APPEARANCES

Two weeks after getting the Minneapolis promotion I started work at the new position. My old boss Peter Lowe drove me to Logan Airport for the flight to Minneapolis. We stopped for a lunch at a restaurant named Jimmies. It was on the Boston Wharf and somewhat exclusive. We were the second of two tables. The other table was a group of about six guys. I noticed that their table was covered in hundred dollar bills. Since I always listened to conversations at the next table it wasn't long before I knew the guys were bookies. Since I knew gambling was illegal in Massachusetts I said to Pete. "We need to call the cops." Pete responded by saying, "See those guys around the table. Those are cops, guarding the bookies."

Lesson: You can't tell a book by its cover. (I cannot believe that I actually said that.)

SALES

LESSON

SILENCE IN NEGOTIATION

When I was a sales guy at Control Data, I worked with a guy named Dick whose job it was to negotiate government contracts. These contracts were very large, worth millions of dollars. His major tool in negotiating these contracts was silence. Dick would sit in silence when the contracting party would ask a question that Dick did not want to answer or had an answer that the contracting party would not like to hear. Dick could sit for minutes in silence. He would wait until the contracting party would break the silence by speaking first, usually moving on to a new topic.

Lesson: Silence is an action.

Psalms 94:11. The LORD knows people's thoughts.

SALES

LESSON

ALL YOU NEED TO KNOW

If you have the answers to the following questions and they all are positive you should get the deal.

Do you have any money?

Are you going to spend this money in my life time?

Would you spend this money with me?

Can my product do the job?

Lesson: Four yeses, and a good strategy, equal a deal

SALES

LESSON

WHO IS IN THE ROOM

Early on in our business history we had changed our name from Microtechnology Resources to Fourth Shift. The software we were developing was for manufacturers and we felt this name reflected better as to who we were. We had also decided to sell our products through third party distributors, i.e. computer stores. There was a chain of stores called Entre'. They had a lot of stores located throughout the Northeast US. The one located in Rochester, New York called saying they had about seventy people who had signed up for a seminar presenting our product's first three modules. Well, we were traveling on our own personal dime so there was some discussion as to whether we should go to present to the group. We decided to go. So, Scot (Ph.D. in manufacturing planning) and I loaded up and headed to Rochester. We got there on a Thursday about mid-day.

Upon arrival, I suggested we gather as many sales folks as we could and call all seventy folks and confirm their attendance. After these calls, about twenty-five folks said they planned to come. Only three guys actually show up. Lots of discussion as to whether we should do the presentation. We decided to do it. About three weeks later, the three that attended called us and bought about twenty-five thousand dollars of our software. Six months later they bought ten million dollars. The three guys were from Kodak and one of them was the gopher for the Executive Vice President of Manufacturing.

Lesson: It's not how many you have in the room but WHO is in the room.

SALES

LESSON

HIGHER POWER

As one of the top sales executives in our company I was often called in to negotiate and close deals. I was called to close a large deal with Detroit Diesel. It was extremely critical because we needed a large down payment to be able to meet the upcoming payroll.

Flying early to Detroit, I had a high expectation of closing the deal and getting the down payment that day or the next. I was expecting to negotiate the deal with one or two people. Well, when I walked into the room there were about a dozen people from Electronic Data Systems (EDS) who had been contracted to run Detroit Diesel's computer resource and negotiate the deal. There was a "drop dead" beautiful woman dressed very smartly who was in charge for their side. It took me about five seconds to realize that she out brained me by a whole bunch. At the proper moment, I said that I felt that I needed my higher power here to help negotiate the deal. I called home office and got Jim on the phone and explained the situation to him. Jim was equally brilliant. The two of us held our own. Two days later we had the deal with the large down payment included. Pay Roll was met.

Lesson: A higher power than you should always be in your sales bag.

Proverbs 13:20. Walk with the wise and become wise.

ENCOUNTERS

ENCOUNTERS

LESSON

AIR TRAVEL: FINDING ELBOW ROOM

When you travel by air frequently you value the aisle seat or window seat. The aisle seat is preferred if you do not like to crawl over someone to go to the restroom. The window is better if you do not like others crawling over you to go to the restroom. The problem is what to do if you get stuck in a middle seat. The is solution I used is:

When stuck in the middle, I would wait until both the window and aisle were occupied. I would then turn to the person in the window seat and say, "Excuse me, are you going to use that barf bag? If not, could I have it?" Then I would turn to the aisle seat person and ask the same question. "Excuse me, are you going to use that barf bag?"

I found that when I had both barf bags the individuals in the aisle and window seat would move immediately. Even stuck in a middle seat, I could always end up having a three seat row by myself.

Lesson: Fool proof method

ENCOUNTERS

LESSON

AIR TRAVEL: CHECK YOURSELF OUT

I was flying to Chicago to make a sales presentation to Abbot Labs. I was in an aisle seat. Next to me was a young lady in her early teens. We weren't ten feet off the ground when she proceeded to puke all over my left side suit coat. I went to the rest room to clean the coat and hoped I would not smell bad. I thought the presentation went well but the people at the conference table seemed nervous. We did the presentation and left for home. When I got home and took my suit coat off I noticed that the underside of the left coat sleeve was covered in puke. So every time I rested my chin on my left hand, the underside of the coat was presented to the table with the vomit covered sleeve. Needless to say, we did not get the order.

Lesson: When someone vomits on you on the way to a sales presentation cancel and go home.

ENCOUNTERS

LESSON

AIR TRAVEL: BOXING

When we lived in Brussels I would fly Sabina to New York's Kennedy. Stayed overnight at Mary's sister and then fly Northwest from New York to Minneapolis the next day. I was first on the flight and dozing in my usual seat, 2-C when I was awakened by someone snapping their fingers in my ear. This irritated me. I awoke with a start and was ready to give the "WHAT TO" to the individual.

When fully turned around, I realized that the individual doing the snapping was Ali. It was Mohammed Ali, World Heavyweight Boxing Champion. When he saw that I was awake, he asked if I would like to see him float like a butterfly. I nodded. He supported himself on the two aisle seats and lifted himself off of the floor. He also showed me some magic tricks, dance steps, and recited poetry.

Lesson: When ready to give the "What To" to somebody, make sure it is not the current heavy weight champ

ENCOUNTERS

LESSON

AIR TRAVEL: EXECUTIVE LOUNGE

We traveled to China from Minneapolis several times. In so doing we would stop in Narita, Japan and change airplanes. As such we would spend an hour or two in the Executive Lounge at the airport while waiting for the next leg of our journey. On one of these trips and in the lounge, I noticed that Henry Kissinger, Nixon's Secretary of State and negotiator of the end of the Viet Nam war was sitting in the lounge. Being me, I went over and thanked him for his service and congratulated him on his brilliant work in negotiating peace with Viet Nam. He was very gracious and expressed his thanks for my thanks. Wonderful time.

Lesson: Even famous people want to be thanked for their great work.

Henry Kissinger, Secretary of State

ENCOUNTERS

LESSON

AIR TRAVEL: BIG GUY, LITTLE GUY

After I had attained about 1.5 million Northwest Airline miles, 2-C became my seat on the airplane. Did not make any difference of the plane type 2-C was my chair. One time flying from Los Angeles to Minneapolis on a DC-ten I thought I was to have a three row seat to myself. Just as they were getting ready to close the door, two guys got on. A really little guy and a big burly type who looked like the bodyguard. They took up the seats right next to me. On the trip, if the little guy wanted something he would whisper in the big guy's ear. The big guy would call the flight attendant to get it. As we were landing at about three thousand feet the two got up and went to the flight attendants jump seat and buckled up. This was highly unusual and to my knowledge illegal. As I was first off after them, I noticed that there was a golf cart waiting for them. The big guy jumped in the driver's seat and the little guy in back. On my way out of the plane I asked, "Who the hell was that??? The flight attendant's response was "Prince".

Lesson: Fame makes allowances.

ENCOUNTERS

LESSON

AIR TRAVEL: LITTLE GUY FOLLOW UP

One week later I was doing the exact same trip, flying L.A. to Minneapolis. This time it was a drop dead beautiful blonde. This attractive blonde sat in first class a few seats back getting all kinds of attention from a fortunate young male seat mate. But, the same routine at the end of the flight. The beautiful blonde got up and went to the flight attendant's jump seat and buckled up. This time I asked the flight attendant who the woman was. Her answer, "Kim Bassinger." I said, "who's she?".

Lesson: Fame can make allowances for others.

VENTURING OUT

VENTURING OUT

LESSON

STARTING A COMPANY

Most people do not try to start their own company, because it is really hard. I was invited to help start a software company with three other guys. I was the sales guy. We were going to write a business application for a microcomputer. The micro had just been introduced. (I know, I know I am aging myself) Surveying the field, we decided to write a manufacturing resource planning system (MRP).

We had each put in a sum of money so we had some operating capital but were actively looking for venture capital (VC).

We had rented a single office with one desk and several chairs for our working space. At this same time two other guys had started a VC company and to get to their office they had to walk through our office. As they did so we would ask if they would like to invest in us. The answer was a clear no.

Always on the job: Ron doing sales and Ian doing customer service

After several tries with other VC's and getting a lot of "no's", we found someone who said they would be lead VC if these two guys would also invest. We got the two parties together who then said yes and we had our start. We had named ourselves Microtechnologies Resources

Lesson: Tenacity is the number one trait needed in starting something worthwhile.

FAITH

FAITH

LESSON

FRIENDSHIP

In the many moves we have always been active in our local church. In four of the moves I have been in a position of leadership within the congregation. The first congregation where I was chairman we were building a church structure. This was in California where land was expensive and real estate agents are generally crazy. It was here that I learned that your pastor could not be your friend, he was your pastor. After we moved to Sudbury, Mass. Harvey Anderson our pastor in California became a friend,

Lesson: Your pastor is not your friend, they are your spiritual shepherd.

Proverbs 17:17. A friend is always loyal, and a brother is born to help in time of need.

FAITH

LESSON

ANSWERED PRAYERS: FAMILY

When my daughter and her fiancé moved to Costa Rica to build a Bed and Breakfast place catering to surfers and folk studying biology for advanced degrees I was very nervous about her and Mike's safety. My servant prayer was that God would send two guardian angels two watch over her and Mike. This was my prayer for many months.

Amy has a deep love for animals and their well-being. When Mary and I went down to Costa Rica for our first visit we meet Kaya and Bear. These were two dogs she adopted which followed her wherever she went in their little village of Puerto Viejo, Costa Rica. Kaya was half Dobermann Pincher and half Great Dane. So what we had here was a huge dog that looked like a Dobermann. When this dog barked the earth shook and people stopped moving. Bear was a frolicking black Lab. Fun. God had sent two angels to watch over Amy and Mike.

Lesson: Prayer works

Proverbs 18:10. The name of the LORD is a strong fortress;

FAITH

LESSON

ANSWERED PRAYERS: FRIENDS

Mary and I had a friend by the name of Barb. She had the gift of hospitality. She lived this gift. She was a widow and yet she would have large groups of people in to her home for an evening of companionship and dinner. Barb took a lot of meds as she had a lot of things wrong with her physically. Her kidneys were failing and near her end here she was in the Apple Valley Health Care facility. I drive for Uber. I had just made a drop off in Rosemount and mentioned to The Lord that it would be great if I could see Barb one more time. The next ride I picked up was a worker at that facility who wanted to be dropped at the exact same door that was the entry to go visit Barb. Dropped him off, turned off the app, and went in to visit Barb. Great visit.

She passed the next day.

Lesson: Prayer works

Proverbs 27:19. As a face is reflected in water, so the heart reflects the real person.

FAITH

LESSON

INSTITUTIONAL CHANGE

As president of our church in Sudbury, Mass. I became intimate with the financial status of our pastor. Even though he was in the retirement program of the denomination he was having a difficult time building a retirement nest egg. We came up with the idea of selling the parsonage to the pastor. The gasps of the folks in the congregation could be heard at great distances. We had some tough sledding in selling the congregation on the idea. Today, a pastor owning their own home is standard practice.

Lesson: New ideas in established institutions can be a really tough sell

FAITH

LESSON

PASTOR'S ARE HUMAN

When we lived in Brussels, Belgium we joined what was named The American Protestant Church. It was a Methodist Mission Church. I became chairman of the church council. While in this position, the pastor hired an American female as assistant pastor. He did this without the normal vetting process or any church council or congregation approval. He related quite the story when defending his decision. He said that without his intervention, this woman would be in poverty and facing starvation. Soon his decision came full circle. The new assistant pastor was driving him crazy and he pleaded with the council to clean up his mess. Needless to say, it was quite an emotional packed situation.

Lesson: Pastors can make mistakes, they're human too.

FAITH

LESSON

GOD'S PREPARATION

The devil is real. When we moved back to the USA from Caracas to Burnsville, Minnesota we joined Faith Covenant church. Again, the Lord tapped my shoulder and I became the council Chair. During this time, the past president was also on the council as a supporter for the new president and to assist in transition to leadership. This individual declared that it was time to fire the current pastor (who had been there for the past twenty plus years) for being a poor administrator. What ensued was incredible and could only be called war. I am convinced that the Lord had been preparing me for this position through the previous three chairmanships. Without going into great detail, I at one point was the only person on the council for not firing the pastor. It was eighteen months of hell on earth. The Lord prevailed and the pastor stayed and the bad guys left.

Lesson: The devil does exist and evil can happen even within a church

Psalm 121:7. The LORD keeps you from all harm and watches over your life.

BUILDING DOWNTOWN BURNSVILLE

BUILDING DOWNTOWN BURNSVILLE

HEART OF THE CITY

Groundbreaking at Grande Market Place

HEART OF THE CITY

LESSON

GOD HAS A WAY

When I retired from Fourth Shift people asked me what I was going to do. I answered by saying that I was going to build downtown Burnsville. This had come to me during an earlier quiet time. I

Grande Market Place

continued to pray about this as I had no idea as to what to do next or even as to what the first step should be. Of course, people smiled when I said I was going to build downtown Burnsville as they knew me as Mr. Sales guy, not as Mr. Developer. After praying about this for many months it came to me to call Dean (a very successful business guy) and Del (a very successful developer). I invited them to my home for breakfast

(Yes Terry in your home as it now stands) and to hear me out. Well both these guys were very enthusiastic about the project.

I told them that from living in England we had noted that people who owned their own retail shops often lived above them. So my idea was to build a downtown area of Burnsville in the European style, retail shops on the first floor with living quarters above them. Dean drew a picture of the development on his paper napkin (no I wasn't smart enough to save it), and Del said he knew where it should be built. After breakfast Del asked me to follow him to the spot. It was a great location. I now had my next steps as suggested by Dean and Del.

Lesson: Pray your way. Talk to the right people. Remember the Kodak story.

HEART OF THE CITY

LESSON

FINDING THE WAY

I needed a professional presentation to use in talking to banks, other developers, or just plain rich people who could fund the project. God lead me to Dave an architect at a downtown Minneapolis firm. Dave owns Buck Hill in Burnsville today. Well with Dave's help and about $15,000 we put together the presentation I used in presenting the project. I started calling it Grande Market Place in, "*The Heart of the City*".

I was making this presentation to a number of people going from bankers and other developers in the later nineties. None were willing to go with me. One developer took the idea of retail and living in one unit in the redevelopment of downtown Hopkins. I wasn't savvy enough for a non-compete agreement. I then had an occasion to make this presentation to Judy, Director of Development for the city of Burnsville. When I got to the part of calling it *The Heart of The City*, Judy about fell out of her chair, the city had just put together a committee to address development of downtown Burnsville and called the committee, *Heart of the City*.

Grande Market Place Business Concept

- Grande Market Place is a destination fashioned after a European village square where the marketplace is the heart of the city.

- Grande Market Place is a place where people gather and want to be. Where you can savor your favorite beverage (in pottery or glass) plan your menu, and shop at the best food ingredient retailers available.

Lesson: To get to this point took about two years of prayer and many missteps. Per Paul you need to run the good race.

GRAND OPENING

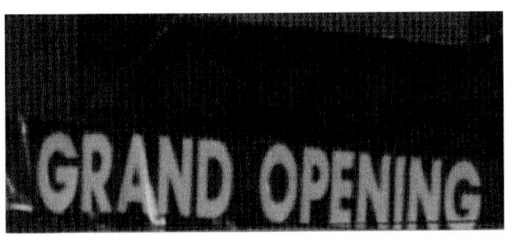

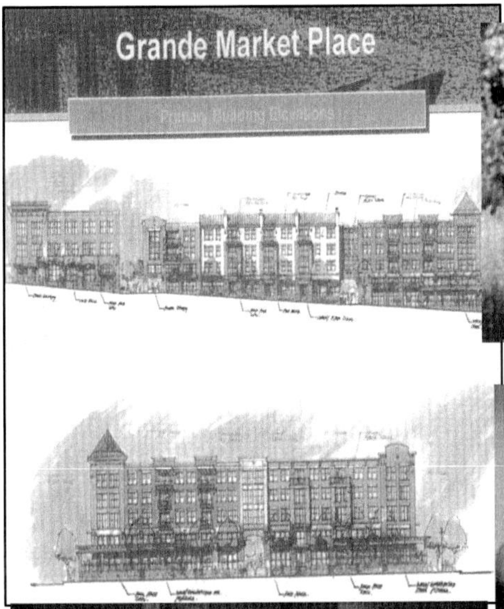
Grande Market Place

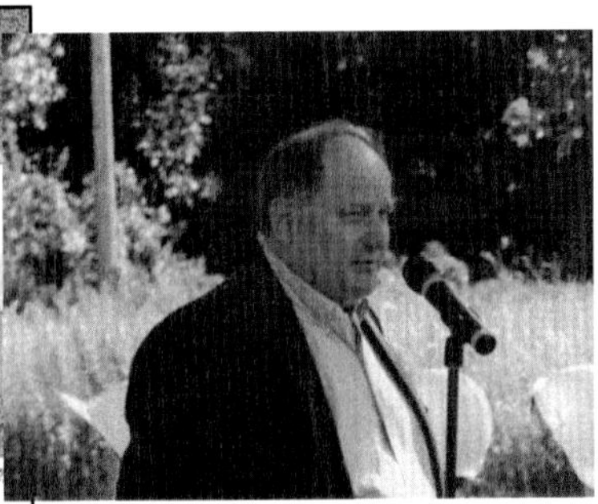

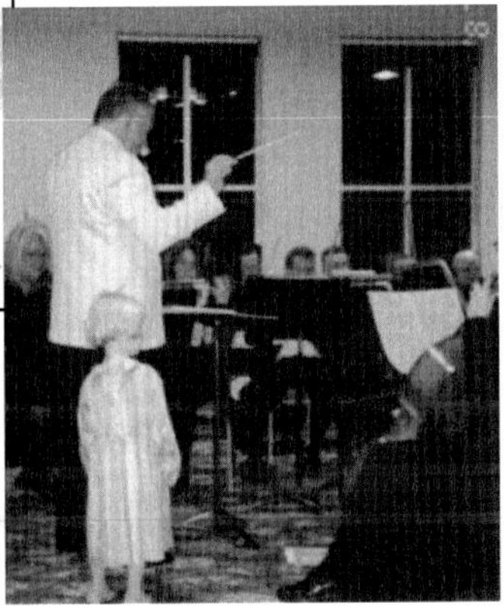

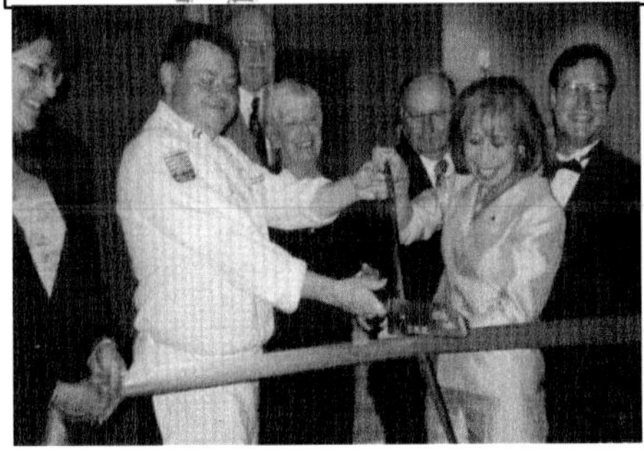

ADVENTURES WITH UBER

ADVENTURES WITH UBER

LESSON

START OF THE DRIVING EXPERIENCE

I am an early riser. I get up between two and three in the early AM. I am also an avid reader. At this early hour I read non-fiction and my Bible. Knowing that I was up folks who knew would call and ask if I could take them to the airport. I would. I did this for years. Then one day Mary (my bride) was talking to one of the ladies who I would take to the airport. During this conversation, the topic of Uber came up. At the end of the conversation the friend stated that "We don't need Uber, we have Ron and he is free." Well Mary came and explained to me that I could get paid to take people to the airport. That was 9000 plus rides ago.

Lesson: There are a lot of ways to make a dollar. (I really said that.)

ADVENTURES WITH UBER

LESSON

MISSION FIELD

As I write this, I have been driving for Uber for five years and have given 9,000 rides. I have learned that whenever I pick someone up or drop them off at a hospital, doctors office, courthouse, police station, rehab center, or hospice care center, I ask if they would like to pray about the circumstances regarding their situation. Everyone that I have asked, save one, have said yes.

Lesson: Driving for Uber is a mission field

Psalm 124:8 Our help is from the LORD, who made heaven and earth.